SAMSUNG GALAXY ULTRA GUIDEBOOK

Mastering Every Feature for Seamless User Experience

Matthew H. Larsen

Copyright

About the Author

The literary world will never be the same without Matthew H. Larsen, a famous author who writes about technology and creativity. Larsen has spent his whole career making complicated technological ideas easy for a wide range of people to understand. He loves figuring out how to use the newest gadgets.

Larsen's writing style is noted for being clear and easy to understand. He has written works that tech experts and people who are just starting out in the field can both relate to because he does a lot of study and has a knack for making complicated things easy to understand. His writing stands out because it breaks down complicated topics into easy-to-understand insights. This makes it a useful resource for people who want to learn how to manage the constantly changing world of technology.

Larsen is a leader in his field and has written a number of well-reviewed guidebooks that show how dedicated he is to making the newest developments easier to understand. Not only are his books complete how-to guides, but they are also helpful companions that help readers get the most out of their gadgets.

Matthew H. Larsen does more than just write. He is also a popular speaker at tech events and conferences, where he shares his knowledge and advice with people who want to stay ahead in the fast-changing tech world. Larsen has an impressive body of work, and he continues to teach and inspire, having a lasting effect on the area where technology and writing meet.

Table of Content

Introduction

- Unveiling the Samsung S24 Ultra

- Purpose of the Guidebook

Chapter 1: Getting Started

- Setting Up Your Samsung Galaxy S24 Ultra

- Navigating the User Interface

Chapter 2: Mastering Features

- Camera Capabilities

- Advanced Display Settings

- Productivity Tools and Apps

Chapter 3: Troubleshooting Tips

- Common Issues and Solutions

- Optimizing Performance

Chapter 4: Customization

- Personalizing Your Samsung S24 Ultra
- Exploring Themes and Widgets

Chapter 5 : Connectivity

- Syncing and Transferring Data
- Connecting to Networks and Devices

Chapter 6: Security and Privacy

- Setting up Biometrics and Security Features
- Protecting Your Privacy

Chapter 7: Tips for Beginners and Seniors

- Simplifying the User Experience
- Enhancing Accessibility Features

Chapter 8: Frequently Asked Questions

- Common Inquiries and Answers

Conclusion

- Summary and Key Takeaways

Introduction

The Samsung Galaxy S24 Ultra, a flagship smartphone that pushes the limits of innovation, is the focal point of this comprehensive guidebook. As technology advances at an unprecedented pace, unveiling the S24 Ultra becomes not just an introduction to a gadget but a journey into the future of mobile technology. This guidebook aims to be your compass, navigating through the intricacies of the Samsung S24 Ultra to empower users with a deep knowledge of its features and functionalitics.

Unveiling the Samsung S24 Ultra:

The Samsung S24 Ultra stands as a pinnacle of engineering and design, having cutting-edge features that redefine the smartphone experience. From its sleek exterior to the advanced technology housed within, this section peels back the layers to show the intricate details of the device. Readers will dig into the device's physical attributes, exploring its display, camera system, and overall build. By unraveling the technological marvels encapsulated in the S24 Ultra, users will gain a greater appreciation for the craftsmanship behind this flagship device.

Purpose of the Guidebook:

Why navigate the S24 Ultra through trial
and error when you can start on your
journey armed with insights and knowledge?
The goal of this guidebook is to serve as a
comprehensive manual, bridging the gap
between users and the full potential of their
Samsung Galaxy S24 Ultra. It goes beyond
the basics, giving a nuanced understanding
of features and functionalities that might go
unnoticed. Whether you're a tech enthusiast
eager to explore every facet of the device or
a newcomer looking for a seamless
onboarding experience, this guidebook
caters to all types of users.

The guidebook's purpose goes beyond a mere exploration of features. It is designed to be a companion, giving practical tips, troubleshooting advice, and customization options to enhance the user experience. By elucidating the purpose of the guidebook, readers are invited to approach the S24 Ultra not just as a gadget but as a tool for productivity, inspiration, and seamless communication.

In the subsequent parts, we will delve into the specifics of setting up and customizing the Samsung S24 Ultra, mastering its features, troubleshooting common issues, and optimizing its performance.

Chapter 1

Getting Started:

Embarking on your journey with the Samsung Galaxy S24 Ultra is an exciting effort. This section serves as your guide, giving step-by-step insights into setting up your device and navigating its user interface. Whether you're unboxing your new phone or trying to optimize your current setup, the following key points will be your compass in the initial stages of your S24 Ultra experience.

1.1　**Setting Up Your Samsung Galaxy S24 Ultra:**

Setting up your Samsung Galaxy S24 Ultra is the important first step towards unlocking its full potential. This subsection provides a full walkthrough of the initial setup process, ensuring a seamless onboarding experience for users of all levels. From powering on the device to configuring important settings, users will find clear instructions and tips to customize their S24 Ultra according to their preferences.

Key Steps:

- Powering on the device and basic configuration.
- Connecting to Wi-Fi and cell networks.

- Setting up biometrics for improved security.

- Configuring Google and Samsung accounts for smooth integration.

- Exploring initial customization possibilities.

Navigating these steps carefully ensures that users not only have a working device but also one tailored to their specific needs and preferences.

1.2 Navigating the User Interface:

Once your Samsung Galaxy S24 Ultra is set up, mastering its user interface is important for a smooth and enjoyable experience. This subsection guides users through the device's interface, from home screens to app navigation, ensuring that every swipe and tap is useful and intuitive.

Key Aspects:

- Screen setup and customization.
- App drawer navigation and management.
- Utilizing the Edge Screen for quick access to apps and tools.
- Exploring widgets and their functions.
- Understanding the notification window and quick settings.

Users gain a comprehensive understanding of how to quickly navigate the S24 Ultra's user interface. The goal is to empower users to make the most out of their interactions with the device.

Chapter 2

Mastering Features:

In this part, we delve into the heart of the Samsung Galaxy S24 Ultra, exploring its standout features that elevate the smartphone experience to new heights. From recording breathtaking moments with advanced camera capabilities to optimizing the display settings and harnessing productivity tools, users will unlock the full potential of their device.

2.1 Camera Capabilities:

The camera system of the Samsung Galaxy S24 Ultra is a technological marvel, and this sub-section is your guide to mastering its powers. From basic photography tips to advanced features, users will discover how to take stunning images and videos.

Key Points:

- Overview of the camera hardware and specs.
- Utilizing the different lenses for various photography scenarios.
- Mastering camera modes: from picture to night mode.
- Exploring advanced functions such as Pro mode and manual controls.
- Tips for improving photography skills and capturing professional-grade shots.

By mastering the camera features, users can turn their Samsung Galaxy S24 Ultra into a strong tool for visual storytelling, preserving memories, and expressing creativity.

2.2 Advanced Display Settings

The S24 Ultra boasts a cutting-edge display, and this sub-section focuses on helping users tailor it to their tastes. From resolution changes to exploring unique display features, users will gain insights into maximizing the visual experience.

Key Aspects:

- Understanding display resolution and refresh rate choices.

- Exploring Adaptive Brightness and Eye Comfort Shield.

- Customizing Edge Lighting for alerts.

- Leveraging Always On Display for at-a-glance details.

- Tips for optimizing display settings based on individual tastes.

By navigating through these advanced display settings, users can ensure that their Samsung Galaxy S24 Ultra not only looks stunning but also matches with their comfort and usability preferences.

2.3 **Productivity Tools and Apps:**

The Samsung Galaxy S24 Ultra goes beyond being a communication gadget; it is a productivity powerhouse. In this sub-section, users will discover a plethora of tools and apps meant to streamline tasks and enhance efficiency.

Key Features:

- Overview of Samsung DeX for desktop-like work.
- Exploring pre-installed work apps and Microsoft integration.
- Tips for working using Split Screen and Pop-up View.
- Utilizing Samsung Notes and other productivity-focused tools.

- Customizing the Edge Panel for quick access to tools.

Mastering these productivity tools and apps turns the S24 Ultra into a versatile companion for work, creativity, and organization. As users delve into this area, they will find their device evolving into a personalized productivity hub, tailored to their unique wants and preferences.

Chapter 3

Troubleshooting Tips:

Even the most advanced devices may face challenges. This section equips users with valuable troubleshooting tips to address common issues and improve the performance of the Samsung Galaxy S24 Ultra. By navigating through these options, users can ensure a seamless and efficient experience with their device.

3.1 Common Issues and Solutions:

This sub-section addresses prevalent challenges users may face and provides practical solutions to resolve them. From connectivity issues to software glitches, users will find advice on troubleshooting common problems that may arise during their S24 Ultra journey.

Common Issues:

- Connectivity trouble with Wi-Fi and mobile networks.
- App crashes and freezing.
- Battery drainage problems.
- Slow speed and lag.
- Touchscreen responsiveness issues.

Solutions:

- Resetting network settings for connection issues.
- Clearing app cache and changing software for app-related problems.
- Optimizing battery usage and finding power-hungry apps.

- Closing background apps and managing storage for performance gains.
- Calibrating the touchscreen for improved responsiveness.

By addressing these common issues proactively, users can keep a smooth and uninterrupted experience with their Samsung Galaxy S24 Ultra.

3.2 Optimizing Performance:

Optimizing the performance of the S24 Ultra means that users can harness its full power. This sub-section offers tips and tricks to enhance the device's speed, responsiveness, and overall efficiency.

Performance Optimization Tips:

- Managing background apps and tasks.

- Utilizing device maintenance tools.

- Adjusting animation options for a snappier experience.

- Monitoring and handling storage space.

- Regularly changing software and firmware.

By incorporating these performance optimization tips into their routine, users can keep their Samsung Galaxy S24 Ultra running at its peak, providing a swift and responsive user experience.

Chapter 4

Customization:

Tailoring your Samsung Galaxy S24 Ultra to suit your tastes is a key aspect of enhancing the overall user experience. In this part, we delve into customization choices, guiding users on how to personalize their device, explore themes, and make the most of widgets.

4.1 Personalizing Your Samsung S24 Ultra:

This sub-section focuses on the myriad ways users can personalize their S24 Ultra, building a device that reflects their style and preferences. From changing wallpapers to tweaking system sounds, users will discover a range of options to make their device truly their own.

Key Customization Options:

- Changing home screen wallpapers and lock screen pictures.
- Customizing system sounds, including ringtones and warning tones.
- Adjusting font styles and sizes for better reading.
- Exploring different image packs for a fresh look.
- Setting up and customizing the Always On Display.

Exploring these personalization options, users can transform their Samsung Galaxy S24 Ultra into a device that not only works exceptionally but also resonates with their individual aesthetic preferences.

4.2 Exploring Themes and Widgets:

Themes and widgets offer a dynamic way to improve the visual appeal and functionality of the Samsung Galaxy S24 Ultra. This sub-section delves into the world of themes, allowing users to change the entire look and feel of their device, as well as widgets, which provide quick access to important information and tools.

Key Aspects:

- Applying and changing pre-installed themes.
- Exploring third-party themes for a diverse range of choices.

- Adding and arranging apps on the home screen.

- Utilizing apps for quick access to weather, calendar, and other information.

- Creating a cohesive visual experience through theme and tool combinations.

By delving into themes and apps, users can truly make their Samsung Galaxy S24 Ultra a personalized and efficient extension of their digital lifestyle.

As users accept the customization options offered by the S24 Ultra, they not only infuse their device with personality but also optimize it for their unique needs. The guidebook continues with exploration into connectivity, security, and tips tailored for beginners and seniors, ensuring a thorough understanding of the Samsung Galaxy S24 Ultra's capabilities.

Chapter 5

Connectivity:

The Samsung Galaxy S24 Ultra is designed to seamlessly connect with different networks and devices, enhancing the overall user experience. In this part, we study the intricacies of connectivity, guiding users through syncing and transferring data, as well as connecting to networks and external devices.

5.1 Syncing and Transferring Data:

Effortless data transfer and synchronization are vital aspects of the S24 Ultra's connectivity features. This sub-section provides a thorough guide on how users can sync their data across devices and efficiently transfer files, ensuring a smooth flow of information.

Key Connectivity Topics:

- Syncing contacts, schedules, and photos with Google and Samsung accounts.

- Utilizing Samsung Cloud for seamless data sharing.

- Transferring information between devices using Bluetooth or USB.

- Exploring wireless choices for data transfer, such as NFC and Samsung Quick Share.

- Backing up and restoring data for added protection.

By mastering these data syncing and transfer methods, users can maintain a cohesive digital ecosystem across their devices, ensuring that their Samsung Galaxy S24 Ultra is an integral part of their connected lifestyle.

5.2 Connecting to Networks and Devices:

The S24 Ultra's connectivity goes beyond personal data to encompass networks and external devices. This sub-section focuses on the various ways users can connect their device to networks for seamless internet access and pair it with other devices for improved functionality.

Key Connectivity Aspects:

- Connecting to Wi-Fi networks and managing saved links.

- Utilizing cell networks for internet access on the go.

- Pairing the S24 Ultra with Bluetooth-enabled devices, such as headphones and speakers.

- Exploring the flexibility of USB connections for file transfer and gadget interaction.

- Understanding and maximizing the promise of 5G connectivity.

With these connectivity features, users can ensure that their Samsung Galaxy S24 Ultra is not only a powerful standalone device but also an integral part of a connected ecosystem, providing them with internet

access and device interactions tailored to
their tastes.

Chapter 6

Security and Privacy:

Ensuring the security and privacy of your data is crucial in today's digital age. This part of the guidebook focuses on the robust security features of the Samsung Galaxy S24 Ultra, guiding users through the setup of biometrics and other security measures, as well as providing insights into protecting their privacy.

6.1 Setting up Biometrics and Security Features:

Biometrics play a crucial role in securing the Samsung Galaxy S24 Ultra, giving users convenient and robust methods to safeguard their device. This sub-section provides step-by-step directions on setting up biometric features and other security measures.

Key Security Features:

- Configuring fingerprint recognition for safe and convenient unlocking.
- Setting up facial recognition for an extra layer of biometric security.
- Exploring secure folder choices for private and confidential files.
- Enabling and customizing device encryption for improved data protection.
- Utilizing security tools such as Find My Mobile for device tracking and remote control.

By adopting these security features, users can fortify their Samsung Galaxy S24 Ultra against unauthorized access and protect their private information.

6.2 **Protecting Your Privacy:**

Beyond biometrics, protecting your privacy includes understanding and managing various settings and features of the S24 Ultra. This sub-section delves into privacy security measures, empowering users to control and secure their personal data.

Key Privacy Protection Strategies:

- Managing app rights for granular control over data access.

- Reviewing and adjusting location choices for privacy-conscious usage.

- Understanding and adjusting privacy settings in Samsung accounts.

- Utilizing secure browsing choices and VPNs for enhanced online privacy.

- Exploring choices for controlling and limiting data sharing.

By actively engaging with these privacy protection strategies, users can foster a sense of trust in the security and privacy of their Samsung Galaxy S24 Ultra, ensuring that their personal information remains confidential.

As users navigate through the security and privacy features, the guidebook continues with a focus on frequently asked questions, summarizing key lessons, and providing journal prompts and workbook exercises for a comprehensive understanding and utilization of the Samsung Galaxy S24 Ultra's capabilities.

Chapter 7

Tips for Beginners and Seniors:

Understanding the needs of both beginners and seniors is important for ensuring a good and inclusive user experience with the Samsung Galaxy S24 Ultra. This section provides practical tips tailored to these user groups, focusing on simplifying the overall user experience and improving accessibility features.

7.1 Simplifying the User Experience:

For beginners, navigating a feature-rich gadget like the Samsung Galaxy S24 Ultra can be overwhelming. This sub-section offers advice on simplifying the user experience, providing tips that ease the learning curve and ensure a smooth transition into the world of smartphones.

Key Tips for Beginners:

- Starting with important apps and features.
- Using guided lessons for a hands-on learning experience.
- Organizing home screens for easy navigation.
- Taking advantage of voice commands for hands-free working.
- Gradually exploring advanced features as familiarity builds.

By following these tips, beginners can build confidence in their interactions with the device, eventually unlocking its full potential at a comfortable pace.

7.2 Enhancing Accessibility Features:

Seniors, like beginners, may benefit from mobility features that cater to specific needs. This sub-section explores the accessibility options available on the Samsung Galaxy S24 Ultra, allowing seniors to adjust the device to suit their tastes and requirements.

Key Accessibility Features:

- Adjusting font size and style for better reading.
- Enabling high contrast or dark mode for better visibility.
- Utilizing voice assistants for hands-free control.
- Exploring one-handed mode for better reachability.
- Customizing gesture settings and touch sensitivity.

By incorporating these accessibility features into their device usage, seniors can enhance the general usability of the Samsung Galaxy S24 Ultra, ensuring a more comfortable and enjoyable experience.

As users, whether beginners or seniors, apply these tailored tips, they can maximize their enjoyment of the Samsung Galaxy S24 Ultra, ensuring that the device adapts to their needs and tastes. The guidebook concludes with commonly asked questions, summarizing key lessons, and providing journal prompts and workbook projects for a comprehensive understanding and application of the smartphone's features.

Chapter 8

Frequently Asked Questions:

Addressing common inquiries is important for users seeking quick solutions and insights. This section compiles commonly asked questions (FAQs) linked to the Samsung Galaxy S24 Ultra, providing clear and concise answers to assist users in resolving common issues and gaining a deeper knowledge of their device.

8.1 **Common Inquiries and Answers:**

Q1: How do I take a picture on the Samsung Galaxy S24 Ultra?

A: To take a screenshot, simultaneously press the power button and volume down button. You can also use palm swipe movements by swiping the edge of your hand across the screen.

Q2: Is the Samsung Galaxy S24 Ultra water-resistant?

A: Yes, the Samsung Galaxy S24 Ultra comes with water and dust resistance, allowing it to withstand immersion in water for a certain time and depth. Ensure all ports are sealed correctly for optimal protection.

Q3: How can I increase the battery life of my S24 Ultra?

A: To optimize battery life, manage background apps, change screen brightness, and enable power-saving modes. Additionally, consider removing unnecessary features like Always On Display when not needed.

Q4: Can I expand the storage of my Samsung Galaxy S24 Ultra?

A: The S24 Ultra allows expandable storage through a microSD card. Locate the card slot (usually near the SIM tray) and insert a compatible microSD card to increase your device's storage capacity.

Q5: How do I update my Samsung Galaxy S24 Ultra's software?

A: Ensure your device is linked to Wi-Fi, go to Settings > Software update > Download and install. The device will check for updates, and you can follow the on-screen directions to install the latest software version.

Q6: What is the aim of the Samsung DeX feature?

A: Samsung DeX lets you to connect your S24 Ultra to a monitor or TV and use it as a desktop-like experience. It's useful for productivity chores, multitasking, and utilizing your phone as a computing hub.

Q7: How can I protect my Samsung Galaxy S24 Ultra in case of loss or theft?

A: Utilize security tools like Find My Mobile for tracking and remotely controlling your device. Ensure that biometrics, private folder, and encryption are set up for an additional layer of protection.

Q8: Can I change the navigation buttons on my S24 Ultra?

A: Yes, you can modify the navigation buttons by going to Settings > Display > Navigation bar. Choose your preferred button layout and change additional settings for a personalized navigation experience.

Q9: What are some tips for taking better photos with the S24 Ultra camera?

A: Experiment with different camera modes, utilize the multiple lenses for varied shots, and take advantage of features like Pro mode for manual controls. Consider exploring third-party camera apps for extra creative options.

Q10: How do I make a factory reset on my Samsung Galaxy S24 Ultra?

A: Go to Settings > General management > Reset > Factory data reset. Follow the on-screen directions, and be aware that this action will erase all data on your device, so ensure you have a backup.

By addressing these frequently asked questions, users can troubleshoot common issues, improve their knowledge of the Samsung Galaxy S24 Ultra, and make the most out of the device's features. The guidebook ends with a summary of key lessons and provides journal prompts and workbook exercises for users to engage in a reflective and hands-on study of their device.

Conclusion

As we end our study of the Samsung Galaxy S24 Ultra through this guidebook, let's recap the key lessons and takeaways that empower users to fully harness the potential of their device.

Summary and Key Takeaways:

1. Unveiling the Samsung S24 Ultra:

The S24 Ultra stands as a pinnacle of style and technology, redefining the smartphone experience.

2. Getting Started:

Setting up the device and mastering the user interface lays the basis for a seamless experience.

3. Mastering Features:

From camera capabilities to advanced display settings, users can discover the full potential of their S24 Ultra.

4. Troubleshooting Tips:

Addressing common issues and optimizing speed ensures a smooth and uninterrupted user experience.

5. Customization:

Personalizing the device through themes and widgets adds a bit of individuality to the S24 Ultra.

6. Connectivity:

Syncing data, connecting to networks, and pairing with devices make a seamlessly connected experience.

7. Security and Privacy:

Setting up biometrics, securing privacy, and utilizing security features are crucial for data safety.

8. Tips for Beginners and Seniors:

Simplifying the user experience and enhancing accessibility features cater to users of all types.

9. Frequently Asked Questions:

Common inquiries are addressed to provide quick answers and insights.

In essence, the Samsung Galaxy S24 Ultra is not just a device; it's a companion that adapts to the needs and tastes of its users. By delving into the guidebook, users gain the knowledge and skills to manage their device easily, troubleshoot challenges effectively, and personalize it for a truly tailored experience.

As technology changes, this guidebook serves as a timeless resource, ensuring users can continually maximize the potential of their Samsung Galaxy S24 Ultra. From capturing memorable moments with the advanced camera system to securing personal data through robust security features, the S24 Ultra is a device that grows with its users, offering a dynamic and enriching digital experience.

www.ingramcontent.com/pod-product-compliance
Lightning Source LLC
Chambersburg PA
CBHW060213260726
48658CB00005BA/2016